The Jumble Sale

by **Barbara Mitchelhill**
illustrated by **Michael Reid**

There was going to be a Jumble Sale at school.

"We are going to have a Jumble Sale at school. Who can help?" said Mr Day.

They all wanted to help.

"I can get some clothes," said Kamal.

"I can get some toys," said Nicky.

"I can get some books," said Jamie.

Nicky went home. He went up in the loft. He looked in a box for some of his old toys. He wanted to take them to the Jumble Sale.

Kamal and Ranjit went home. Kamal saw some old clothes.

"Can I take them to the Jumble Sale?" she said to Mum.

Hope went home. She saw Dad's old chair. Dad didn't want Hope to take it. He said she could have the bike. It was very old!

Beth went home. She saw some old books. She wanted to take them to the Jumble Sale. Her mum said she could have them.

They all went off to school for the Jumble Sale.

"What have you got?" said Beth.

"I've got some old toys," said Nicky.

Nicky took some toys. Kamal and Ranjit took some old clothes. Jamie and Beth took some old books. Hope took the old bike.

"Where can I put my toys?" said Nicky.

"Put them on that table," said Mr Day.

"Can we help?" said Hope.

Mr Day said that they could help.

But Beth didn't help — she had a book under the table. And Jamie didn't help — he had some roller skates!

They all saw Jamie on his roller skates. He didn't see Beth. She got in the way and Jamie fell over.

Mr Day helped Jamie. Jamie had to take off his jumper so Mr Day could look at his arm.

Some mums and dads wanted to come to the Jumble Sale. Mr Day said Ranjit could let them in.

The mums and dads came to the Jumble Sale. Beth saw her mum and Jamie saw his dad.

They all helped with the Jumble Sale.

A girl wanted one of Nicky's toys.

A boy wanted one of Beth's books. Beth wanted the bike! Mr Day said she could have it.

“That was a good Jumble Sale,” said Hope.

“Yes, it was,” said Mr Day.

It was a good Jumble Sale.

Jamie wanted his jumper. Mr Day said it was on the table but Jamie could not see it.

"Can you see Jamie's jumper?" said Mr Day.

They all looked for Jamie's jumper.

They looked *on* the tables ...

they looked *under* the tables ...

but they couldn't see it.

Beth's mum came to take her home.
Beth said she was looking for
Jamie's jumper.

Beth's mum had Jamie's jumper. She got it at the Jumble Sale.

"Here you are, Jamie," she said.

It's good to have my jumper!
50p